Spirit of Play
SOCCER

Theresa S. Halzle

Augsburg Books
MINNEAPOLIS

W9-BIO-989

SPIRIT OF PLAY: SOCCER

Large-quantity purchases or custom editions of this book are available at a discount from the publisher. Fe
more information, contact the sales department at Augsburg Fortress, Publishers, 1-800-328-4648, or write t
Sales Director, Augsburg Fortress, Publishers, P.O. Box 1209, Minneapolis, MN 55440-1209.

Also distributed by ACTA Publications, 4848 North Clark Street, Chicago, IL 60640-4711

ISBN 0-8066-4584-9

Cover design by Laurie Ingram Design; book design by Michelle L. N. Cook

The paper used in this publication meets the minimum requirements of American National Standard fc
Information Sciences—Permanence of Paper for Printed Library Materials, ANSI Z329.48-1984. ♾ ™

Manufactured in Canada

07   06   05   04   03   1   2   3   4   5   6   7   8   9   10

Then he took the Book of the Covenant and read it to the people.

—Exodus 24:7 NIV

My prayer is that the light will flood your hearts and that you will understand the hope that was given to you when God chose you. Then you will discover the glorious blessings that will be yours together with all of God's people.

—Ephesians 1:18-20 CEV

I press toward the goal for the prize of the upward call of God in Christ Jesus.

—Philippians 3:14 NKJV

In times of trouble I pray to the Lord;
all night long I lift my hands in prayer,
but I cannot find comfort.

—Psalm 77:2 TEV

The Spirit himself testifies with our spirit
that we are God's children.
Now if we are children,
then we are heirs—heirs of God
and co-heirs with Christ,
if indeed we share in his sufferings
in order that we may also share
in his glory.

—Romans 8:16-17 NIV

But He knows the way that I take;
when He has tested me,
I shall come forth as gold.
My foot has held fast to His steps;
I have kept His way and not turned aside.

—Job 23:10-11 NKJV

He gives power to the weak, and to those
who have no might He increases strength.
Even the youths shall faint and be weary,
and the young men shall utterly fall,
but those who wait on the Lord
shall renew their strength;
They shall mount up with wings like eagles,
they shall run and not be weary,
they shall walk and not faint.

—Isaiah 40:29–31 NKJV

All of you are people who belong to the light,
who belong to the day. We do not belong
to the night or to the darkness.
So then, we should not be sleeping
like the others;
we should be awake and sober.
                    —1 Thessalonians 5:5-6 TEV

Finally, let the mighty strength
of the Lord make you strong.
—Ephesians 6:10 CEV

Though you have not seen him, you love him; and even though you do not see him now, you believe in him and are filled with an inexpressible and glorious joy, for you are receiving the goal of your faith, the salvation of your souls.

—1 Peter 1:8-9 NIV

Then said I: "Ah, Lord God! Behold, I cannot speak, for I am a youth." But the Lord said to me: "Do not say, 'I am a youth,' for you shall go to all to whom I send you, and whatever I command you, you shall speak."
—Jeremiah 1:6-7 NKJV

Let us keep our eyes fixed on Jesus, on whom
our faith depends from beginning to end.
He did not give up because of the cross!
On the contrary, because of the joy
that was waiting for him,
he thought nothing of the disgrace of dying
on the cross, and he is now seated
at the right side of God's throne.
Think of what he went through;
how he put up with so much hatred
from sinners! So do not let yourselves
become discouraged and give up.

—Hebrews 12:2-3 TEV

Be strong in the Lord and
in the power of His might.
—Ephesians 6:10 NKJV

God's spirit doesn't make cowards out of us. The Spirit gives us power, love, and self-control.
—2 Timothy 1:7 CEV

Have mercy on me, O Lord,
for I am weak;
O Lord, heal me,
for my bones are troubled.

—Psalm 6:2 NKJV

Hear my cry, O God;
listen to my prayer!
In despair and far from home
I call to you!
Take me to a safe refuge,
for you are my protector,
my strong defense against my enemies.
—Psalm 61:1-3 TEV

For we are God's workmanship,
created in Christ Jesus to do good works,
which God prepared in advance for us to do.
—Ephesians 2:10 NIV

With all my heart, I will praise the Lord.
Let all who are helpless, listen and be glad.
Honor the Lord with me!
Celebrate his great name.

—Psalm 34:2-3 CEV

We then who are strong ought to bear with the scruples of the weak, and not to please ourselves. Let each of us please his neighbor for his good, leading to edification.

—Romans 15:1-2 NKJV

He keeps the law of his God in his heart and never departs from it.

—Psalm 37:31 TEV

I have no greater joy than to hear that
my children are walking in the truth.
—3 John 1:4 NIV

My little group of
disciples, don't be
afraid! Your Father
wants to give you
the kingdom.
—Luke 12:32 CEV

Therefore we also, since we are surrounded
by so great a cloud of witnesses,
let us lay aside every weight,
and the sin which so easily ensnares us,
and let us run with endurance
the race that is set before us.

—Hebrews 12:1 NKJV

Remember this, my dear brothers! Everyone must be quick to listen, but slow to speak and slow to become angry. Man's anger does not achieve God's righteous purpose.
—James 1:19–20 TEV

The Lord delights in the way of the man
whose steps he has made firm;
though he stumble, he will not fall,
for the Lord upholds him with his hand.
—Psalm 37:23-24 NIV

You have taught me since I was a child,
and I never stop telling
about your marvelous deeds.
—Psalm 71:17 CEV

But by the grace of God I am what I am, and His grace toward me was not in vain; but I labored more abundantly than they all, yet not I, but the grace of God which was with me.

—1 Corinthians 15:10 NKJV

You may make your plans, but God directs your actions.

—Proverbs 16:9 TEV

This is love for God: to obey his commands.
And his commands are not burdensome,
for everyone born of God has overcome the world.
This is the victory that has overcome the world,
even our faith. Who is it that overcomes the world?
Only he who believes that Jesus is the Son of God.

—1 John 5:3-5 NIV

Think how much the Father loves us.
He loves us so much that he lets us be called
his children, as we truly are.
But since the people of this world
did not know who Christ is,
they don't know who we are.
My dear friends, we are already God's children,
though what we will be hasn't yet been seen.
But we do know that when Christ returns,
we will be like him,
because we will see him as he truly is.
This hope makes us keep ourselves holy,
just as Christ is holy.

—1 John 3:1-3 CEV

Therefore I will look to the Lord;
I will wait for the God of my salvation;
My God will hear me.

—Micah 7:7 NKJV